Crime

Introduction To Criminology And Some Theories That Will Help Recognize Crime

Copyright © 2020

All rights reserved.

DEDICATION

The author and publisher have provided this e-book to you for your personal use only. You may not make this e-book publicly available in any way. Copyright infringement is against the law. If you believe the copy of this e-book you are reading infringes on the author's copyright, please notify the publisher at: https://us.macmillan.com/piracy

Contents

Introduction To Criminology 1

Classical And Rational Choice Theory 16

Positivist Theory 26

Strain Theories 34

Psychological Theories of Crime 68

Recognize the Signs That Someone Is Lying 73

Introduction To Criminology

Criminology is the study of crime and criminals, including the causes, prevention, correction, and impact of crime on society. Since it emerged in the late 1800s as part of a movement for prison reform, criminology has evolved into a multidisciplinary effort to identify the root causes of crime and develop effective methods for preventing it, punishing its perpetrators, and mitigating its effect on victims.

Key Takeaways: Criminology

- Criminology is the scientific study of crime and criminals.

- It involves research to identify the factors that motivate certain persons to commit crimes, the impact of crime on society, the punishment of crime, and the development of ways to prevent it.
- People involved in criminology are called criminologists and work in law enforcement, government, private research, and academic settings.
- Since its beginnings in the 1800s, criminology has evolved into an ongoing effort to help law enforcement and the criminal justice system respond to the changing societal factors contributing to criminal behavior.
- Criminology has helped develop several effective modern crime prevention practices such as community-oriented and predictive policing.

Criminology Definition

Criminology (from Latin crimen, "accusation", and Ancient Greek -λογία, -logia, from λόγος logos meaning: "word, reason") is the study of crime and deviant behavior.[citation needed] Criminology is an interdisciplinary field in both the behavioural and social sciences, which draws primarily upon the research of sociologists, psychologists, philosophers, psychiatrists, biologists, s ocial anthropologists, as well as scholars of law.

The term criminology was coined in 1885 by Italian law professor Raffaele Garofalo as Criminologia. Later, French anthropologist Paul Topinard used the analogous French term Criminologie [fr].[1] Paul Topinard's major work appeared in 1879. In the eighteenth and early nineteenth centuries, the emphasis of criminology was on the reform of criminal law and not on the causes of crime. Scholars such as Cesare Beccaria and Jeremy Bentham, were more concerned with the humanitarian aspects in dealing with criminals and reforming several criminal laws. Great progress in criminology was made after the first quarter of the twentieth century. The first American textbook on criminology was written in 1920 by sociologist Maurice Parmalee under the title Criminology. Programmes were developed for the specific purpose of training students to be criminologists, but the development was rather slow

Criminology encompasses a wider analysis of criminal behavior, as opposed to the general term crime, which refers to specific acts, such as robbery, and how those acts are punished. Criminology also attempts to account for fluctuations in crime rates due to changes in society and law enforcement practices. Increasingly, criminologists working in law enforcement employ advanced tools of scientific forensics, such as fingerprint study, toxicology, and DNA analysis to detect, prevent, and more often than not, solve crimes.

Modern criminology seeks a deeper understanding of the psychological and sociological influences that make certain people more likely than others to commit crimes.

From a psychological perspective, criminologists attempt to explain how deviant personality traits—such as a constant need for the gratification of desires—might trigger criminal behavior. In doing so, they study the processes by which people acquire such traits and how their criminal response to them can be restrained. Often, these processes are attributed to the interaction of genetic predisposition and repeated social experiences.

Many theories of criminology have come from the study of deviant behavioral sociological factors. These theories suggest that criminality is a natural response to certain types of social experiences.

History

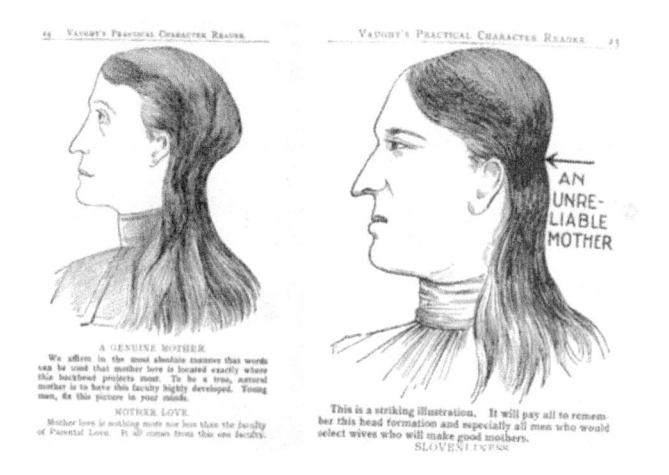

Early criminology attempts to connect physical characteristics to criminal behavior. Corbis Historical / Getty Images

The study of criminology began in Europe during the late 1700s when concerns arose over the cruelty, unfairness, and inefficiency of the prison and criminal court system. Highlighting this early so-called classical school of criminology, several humanitarians such as Italian jurist Cesare Beccaria and British lawyer Sir Samuel Romilly sought to reform the legal and correctional systems rather than the causes of the crime itself. Their primary goals were to reduce the use of capital punishment, humanize prisons, and compel judges to follow the principles of due process of law.

In the early 1800s, the first annual statistical reports on crime were published in France. Among the first to analyze these statistics, Belgian mathematician and sociologist Adolphe Quetelet discovered certain repeating patterns in them. These patterns included items such as the types of crimes committed, the number of people accused of crimes, how many of them were convicted, and the distribution of criminal offenders by age and gender. From his studies, Quetelet concluded that "there must be an order to those things which…are reproduced with astonishing constancy, and always in the same way." Quetelet would later argue that societal factors were the root cause of criminal behavior.

Cesare Lombroso

Cesare Lombroso (1836-1909), Italian physician and criminologist. Bettmann

During the late 1800s and early 1900s, Italian physician Cesare Lombroso, known as the father of modern criminology, began studying the characteristics of criminals in hopes of learning why they committed crimes. As the first person in history to apply scientific methods in crime analysis, Lombroso initially concluded that criminality was inherited and that criminals shared certain physical characteristics. He suggested that persons with certain skeletal and neurological abnormalities such as close-set eyes and brain tumors were "born criminals" who, as biological throwbacks, had failed to evolve normally. Like American biologist Charles Davenport's 1900s theory of eugenics suggesting that genetically inherited characteristics such as race could be used to predict criminal behavior, Lombroso's theories were controversial and eventually largely discredited by social scientists. However, like Quetelet before him, Lombroso's research had attempted to identify the causes of crime—now the goal of modern criminology.

Modern Criminology

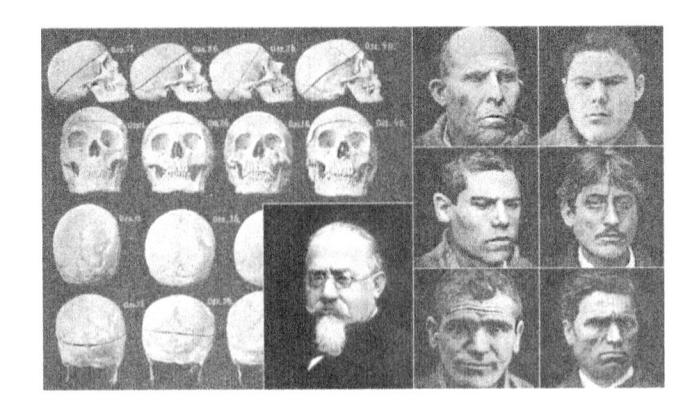

Modern criminology in the United States evolved from 1900 to 2000 in three phases. The period from 1900 to 1930, the so-called "Golden Age of Research," was characterized by the multiple-factor approach, the belief that crime is caused by a multitude of factors that cannot readily be explained in general terms. During the "Golden Age of Theory" from 1930 to 1960, the study of criminology was dominated by Robert K. Merton's "strain theory," stating that the pressure to achieve socially accepted goals—the American Dream—triggered most criminal behavior. The final period from 1960 to 2000, brought extensive, real-world testing of predominant criminological theories using generally empirical methods. It was the research conducted during this last phase that brought about the fact-based theories on crime and criminals applied today.

FBI criminologist examines fingerprints

The formal teaching of criminology as a distinct discipline, separate from criminal law and justice, began in 1920 when sociologist Maurice Parmelee wrote the first American textbook on criminology, titled simply Criminology. In 1950, famed former Berkeley, California, chief of police August Vollmer founded America's first school of criminology specifically to train students to be criminologists on the campus of the University of California, Berkeley.

Modern criminology encompasses the study of the nature of crime and criminals, the causes of crime, the effectiveness of criminal laws, and the functions of law enforcement agencies and correctional institutions. Drawing on both the natural and social sciences, criminology attempts to separate pure from applied research and statistical from intuitive approaches to problem-solving.

Today, criminologists working in law enforcement, government, private research companies, and academia, apply cutting-edge science and technology to better understand the nature, causes, and effects of crime. Working with local, state, and federal legislative bodies, criminologists help create policy dealing with crime and punishment. Most visible in law enforcement, criminologists have helped develop and apply techniques of modern policing and crime prevention such as community-oriented policing and predictive policing.

Criminological Theories

The focus of modern criminology is criminal behavior and the contributing biological and sociological factors that cause rising crime rates. Just as society has changed over criminology's four century-long history, so too have its theories.

Biological Theories of Crime

The earliest effort to identify the causes of criminal behavior, the biological theories of crime state that certain human biological characteristics, such as genetics, mental disorders, or physical condition, determine whether or not an individual will have a tendency to commit criminal acts.

Classical Theory: Emerging during the Age of Enlightenment, classical criminology focused more on the fair and humane punishment of crime than on its causes. Classical theorists believed that humans exercised free will in making decisions and that as "calculating animals," would naturally avoid behaviors that caused them pain. They thus believed that the threat of punishment would deter most people from committing crimes.

Positivist Theory: Positivist criminology was the first study of the causes of crime. Conceived by Cesare Lombroso in the early 1900s, positivist theory rejected the classical theory's premise that people make rational choices to commit crimes. Instead, positive theorists believed that certain biological, psychological, or sociological abnormalities are the causes of crime.

General Theory: Closely related to his positivist theory, Cesare Lombroso's general theory of crime introduced the concept of criminal atavism. In the early stages of criminology, the concept of atavism—an evolutionary throwback—postulated that criminals shared physical features similar to those of apes and early humans, and as "modern savages" were more likely to act in ways contrary to the rules of modern civilized society.

Sociological Theories of Crime

A majority of criminological theories have been developed since 1900 through sociological research. These theories assert that individuals who are otherwise biologically and psychologically normal will naturally respond to certain social pressures and circumstances with criminal behavior.

Cultural Transmission Theory: Arising in the early 1900s, the cultural transmission theory contended that criminal behavior is transmitted from generation to generation—a "like father, like son" concept. The theory suggested that certain shared cultural beliefs and values in some urban areas spawn traditions of criminal behavior that persist from one generation to another.

Strain Theory: First developed by Robert K. Merton in 1938, strain theory stated that certain societal strains increase the likelihood of crime. The theory held that the emotions of frustration and anger arising from dealing with these strains create pressure to take corrective action, often in the form of crime. For example, people undergoing chronic unemployment may be tempted to commit theft or drug dealing to obtain money.

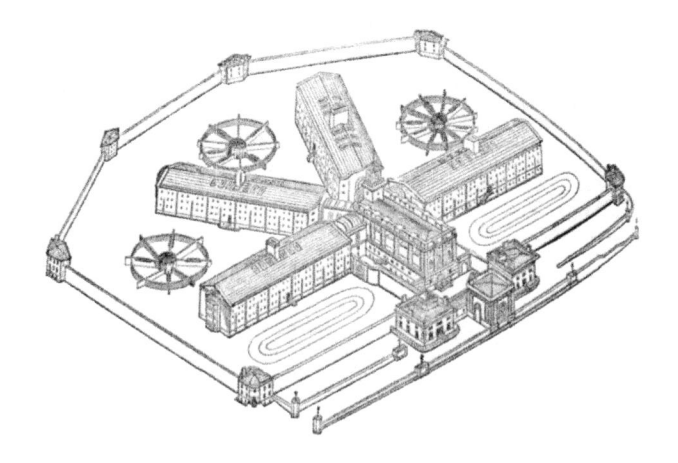

Social Disorganization Theory: Developed after the end of World War II, the social disorganization theory asserted that the sociological characteristics of peoples' home neighborhoods contribute substantially to the likelihood that they will engage in criminal behavior. For example, the theory suggested that especially in disadvantaged neighborhoods, young people are trained for their future careers as criminals while participating in subcultures that condone delinquency.

Labeling Theory: A product of the 1960s, the labeling theory asserted that an individual's behavior may be determined or influenced by the terms commonly used to describe or classify them. Constantly calling a person a criminal, for instance, can cause them to be treated negatively, thus triggering their criminal behavior. Today, labeling theory is often equated to discriminatory racial profiling in law enforcement.

Routine Activities Theory: Developed in 1979, routine activities theory suggested that when motivated criminals encounter inviting unprotected victims or targets, crimes are likely to occur. It further suggested that some peoples' routine of activities makes them more vulnerable to being viewed as suitable targets by a rationally calculating criminal. For example, routinely leaving parked cars unlocked invites theft or vandalism.

Broken Windows Theory: Closely related to the routine activities theory, the broken window theory stated that visible signs of crime, anti-social behavior, and civil disorder in urban areas create an environment that encourages further, ever more serious crimes. Introduced in 1982 as part of the community-oriented policing movement, the theory suggested that stepped-up enforcement of minor crimes such as vandalism, vagrancy, and public intoxication helps prevent more serious crimes in urban neighborhoods.

Crime

Classical And Rational Choice Theory

Classical criminology usually refers to the work of 18th-century philosophers of legal reform, such as Beccaria and Bentham, but its influence extends into contemporary works on crime and economics and on deterrence, as well as into the rational choice perspective. The entire range of social phenomena can be understood more or less accurately using models of economic transactions and the assumption that people make rational choices between opportunities to maximize their own utility. This was a foundational assumption of classical criminology.

Rational Choice Theory and Get-Tough Policies

Drawing on the classical contention that man is a calculating creature, rational choice criminology begins with the assumption that behaviors of groups and individuals will reflect attempts to maximize pleasure and minimize pain. Theorists in this tradition hypothesize how varying conditions shaping the payoff of an endeavor in combination with varying utilities and desires will contribute to aggregate and individual levels of crime. Most adherents agree that the utilities, or desirability, of activities are varying and subjective, so that crime may have attraction for some people that is not seen by others. There also is widespread agreement that the strength and quality of individual or group preferences can be taken into account in studying the occurrence of criminal behavior. Therefore, in criminology rational choice theory usually is a variant of expected utility theories and portrays the process of considering (or ignoring) criminal opportunities as part of a rational calculation based in part on subjective assessments wherein the expected costs and benefits of actions are considered.

The fundamental assumptions and methods associated with rational choice theory and its classical predecessor undergird a great deal of modern criminology, but its theoretical proponents and defenders have been in and out of fashion throughout criminology's history. The perspective fell from favor in the eyes of many criminologists in the last several decades in part because of its resonance with audiences prepared to "get tough" on crime through mass imprisonment and in part because it was seen as an attack on sociological, psychological, cultural, and structural explanations. It was often portrayed as a reductionist and simplistic theory due to the fact that proponents often emphasized the most obvious costs and benefits of crime commission, such as monetary payoff versus terms of imprisonment. Moreover, its foundational assumptions sometimes are critiqued for being so broad as to be meaningless. In very recent years, however, the theory has attracted investigators drawn by its potential for making clear sense of why people commit crime and its ability to communicate the theoretical reasons behind research results to any audience. In contemporary forms, it also can conveniently integrate structural and perceptual models of offending, and the perspective easily makes sense of the use of a wide array of variables from multiple levels of analysis. The rational choice framework has great capacity for incorporating knowledge and techniques garnered from across the social sciences, because its central premises are extremely broad and conflict directly with few extant statements from other perspectives. In broad form, the rational choice perspective has as much potential for integrating knowledge from various spheres of criminology as does any other grand theory. For all its shortcomings, which derive mainly from economic assumptions about human and aggregate decision making and the tendency to focus on the most tangible variables, it makes efficient sense of complex questions.

Accompanying a more even-keeled political approach and more rigorous empiricism in criminology than was prevalent in more ideologically combative times has been a realization that there is nothing necessarily punitive in classical or rational choice theory and that therefore the perspectives should not be faulted when it is misapplied or misunderstood. Articles framed by the perspectives usually examine the possibility that punishment reduces crime, and often that is found to be the case in at least some examined conditions. However, for people who would use the perspectives as ideology to support getting tough on crime, the approach has as many inherent inconsistencies as convergences. Contemporary versions of rational choice specify countless complications of simple postulated relationships between increased punishment and decreased crime, for example. There clearly the rational choice tradition acknowledges that there are limited conditions under which one should expect punishment increases to lead to reductions in rates of crime or to impede individual decisions to commit crime.

Indeed, people who would turn to rational choice and classical theory for endorsement of punitive perspectives should know that they have opened themselves to attack from their desired theoretical bedfellows. This is because rational choice theorists and their classical forebears generally demand consistent and logical economic arguments and real evidence for the practicality and efficacy of state practices. Those who follow the tradition would evaluate the net payoff of punitive programs skeptically before determining them legitimate. Moreover, the tradition is closely coupled historically with utilitarian views of law wherein good laws are only those that can be enforced (which usually requires considerable popular legitimacy) and that lead to the general betterment. The latter, of course, is a difficult philosophical and empirical obstacle to surmount for people who argue that more punishment is needed.

The earliest classical theorists postulated that many punishments were necessarily irrational and excessive simply because they would inevitably be ineffective in deterring crime. This fact still exerts significant influence in both rational choice and classical theorizing. Laws that are groundless, inefficacious, unprofitable, or needless are not good laws. If any convenient liaison between the classical, rational choice perspective and get-tough policies existed, it seems to have been temporary and probably not all that important for, properly modified, almost any broad ideology can inspire or be used to defend vengeful approaches to criminal justice.

Classical and Rational Choice Theorists and Their Heirs

Because the intellectual seeds for classical and rational choice criminology were sown in the 18th-century Enlightenment Age, many of the central questions and biases in the approaches were formed then. When the theories are recapped in textbooks, one is as likely to see reference to Beccaria and Bentham as to lesser sociological thinkers on choice and economics of crime of the last half century. Although the mathematics in contemporary applications sometimes are overwhelming to people who are unaccustomed to reading formulas, the thinking in older and newer versions of classical criminology at least is familiar. Much in the U.S. system of justice rests on the same foundations, and we live with the cultural and intellectual legacy spawned by the scholars who inspired classical criminology. The most important historical fact to keep in mind is that classical theorists were concerned primarily with reforming a primitive, irrational justice system that often was based on privilege and vengeful ritualistic traditions with a justice system that drew legitimacy from reason.

Early classical theorists knew that crime required rational management; they intended to calibrate the law and justice system for the task and generally agreed that the state should do no more than required to protect citizens and their property. The law should be pragmatic and effective. Precise visions of the philosophical underpinnings of rights, the law, and justice varied widely, but there was near-universal agreement among classical and enlightened thinkers of the 18th century that the deterrent value of the law should expend the least possible harm to society and to the individual; that is, the law should operate without undue or unneeded cruelty to offenders. According to this perspective, the costs of committing a given crime usually would slightly outweigh potential benefits, in order to tip the decisional scales toward compliance with the law; however, any punishment beyond that needed to accomplish this task is likely cruel and unnecessary. Classical visions eventually came to reflect the utilitarian ideas that balancing private and individual interests against public interest required optimizing liberty; minimizing harm; and, wherever possible, close correspondence between the two objectives. From inception, theorists contended that implementing rational law and legal measures required dispassionate judgment of what would be most effective and scientific evaluation of attempted improvements. Crime control should be measured and its effectiveness evaluated objectively to ensure the proper balance of controllable costs and benefits of crime. Therefore, most evaluation research of legal changes and large-scale policy changes in the criminal justice system can be comfortably placed under the classical/rational choice tent.

The battles between those who rigidly adhered to purist sociological theories of crime (which generally focused on what is wrong with societies or other external social forces producing aberrant-thinking criminals) and those who took the side of a purist economics and rigid classical criminology are fading to intellectual history. As the latest generation of seasoned combatant in the fight leaves the field, one finds that their legacy is empirical support for multiple approaches to the problem of crime. It educates about the pitfalls of stringent and egotistical adherence to a single perspective and rigid defense of boundaries as much as it provides support for competing visions. With resulting invigorated faith in integration and cross-disciplinary approaches in criminology, rational choice and classical perspectives are on the cusp of revitalization and the perspective that may lead the way in sophisticated and integrated crime theorizing that is to come. The form of rational choice perspectives of the future will starkly contrast with the depictions of the school of thought that were presented in academic critiques and textbook accounts over the last several decades; these often pointed out that the theory was elementary and that it offered an unrealistic or artificial depiction of criminal choice as a rational/ economic outcome.

Positivist Theory

The Positivist School was founded by Cesare Lombroso and was led by two others; Enrico Ferri and Raffaele Garofalo. In criminology, the **Positivist School** has attempted to find scientific objectivity for the measurement and quantification of criminal behavior. The Positivist School had a method that was developed by observing the characteristics of criminals to observe what may be the root cause of their behavior or actions. Since the Positivist's school of ideas came around, the research revolved around its ideas has aided in identifying some of the key differences between those that are "criminals" and those that are not. As the scientific method became the major paradigm in the search for knowledge, the Classical School's social philosophy was replaced by the quest for scientific laws that would be discovered by experts. It is divided into Biological, Psychological and Social.

Biological positivism

If Charles Darwin's Theory of evolution was scientific as applied to animals, the same approach should be applied to "man" as an "animal". Darwin's theory of evolution stated that new species would evolve by the process of evolution. It meant that creatures would adapt to their surroundings and from that, a new species would be created over time. Biological positivism is a theory that takes an individual's characteristics and behavior that make up their genetic disposition is what causes them to be criminals. Biological positivism in theory states that individuals are born criminals and some are not.

Physical characteristics

Historically, medicine became interested in the problem of crime, producing studies of physiognomy (see Johann Kaspar Lavater and Franz Joseph Gall) and the science of phrenology which linked attributes of the mind to the shape of the brain as reveal through the skull. These theories were popular because they absolved society and any failures of its government of responsibility for criminal behavior. The problem lay in the propensities of individual offenders who were biologically distinguishable from law-abiding citizens. This theme was amplified by the Italian School and through the writings of Cesare Lombroso (see L'Uomo Delinquente, The Criminal Man and Anthropological criminology) which identified physical characteristics associated with degeneracy demonstrating that criminals were atavistic throwbacks to an earlier evolutionary form. Charles Goring (1913) failed to corroborate the characteristics but did find criminals shorter, lighter and less intelligent, i.e. he found criminality to be "normal" rather than "pathological" (cf the work of Hooton found evidence of biological inferiority). William Sheldon identified three basic body or somatotypes (i.e. endomorphs, mesomorphs, and ectomorphs), and introduced a scale to measure where each individual was placed. He concluded that delinquents tended to mesomorphy. Modern research might link physical size and athleticism and aggression because physically stronger people have the capacity to use violence with less chance of being hurt in any retaliation. Otherwise, such early research is no longer considered valid. The development of genetics has produced another potential inherent cause of criminality, with chromosome and other genetic factors variously identified as significant to select heredity rather than environment as the cause of crime (see: nature versus nurture). However, the evidence from family, twin, and adoption studies shows no conclusive empirical evidence to prefer either cause.

Intelligence

There are a number of reputable studies that demonstrate a link between lower intelligence and criminality. But the evidence is equivocal because studies among the prison population simply test those criminals actually caught, which might be because they failed to plan the crimes properly or because they were unable to resist interrogation techniques and admitted their crimes. If their intelligence is poor, they are also less likely to be deterred. Emotional intelligence has also been closely related to aggression and criminals. People who tend to have a lower emotional intelligence are those that have a hard time managing their emotions and are more prone to act out and perpetrate criminal behavior.

Other medical factors

Testosterone and adrenaline have been associated with aggression and violence, and the arousal and excited state associated with them. The excessive consumption of alcohol can lower blood sugar levels and lead to aggressiveness, and the use of chemicals in foods and drinks has been associated with hyper-activity and some criminal behaviour.

Psychological positivism

Sigmund Freud divided the personality into the id, the primitive biological drives, the superego, the internalised values, and the ego, memory, perception, and cognition. He proposed that criminal behaviour is either the result of mental illness or a weak conscience. John Bowlby proposed an attachment theory in which maternal deprivation was a factor that might lead to delinquency.

This has been discounted in favour of general privation (Michael Rutter: 1981) or "broken homes" (Glueck: 1950) in which absentee or uncaring parents tend to produce badly behaved children.

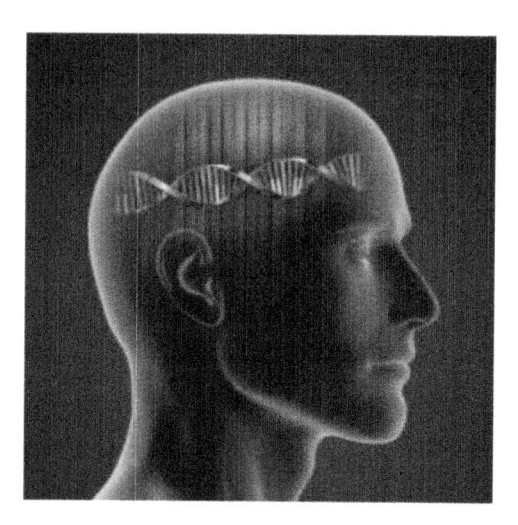

Hans Eysenck (1987) stated that, "...certain types of personality may be more prone to react with anti-social or criminal behaviour to environmental factors of one kind or another." He proposed three dimensions of personality: introversion/extroversion, neuroticism, and psychoticism. For these purposes, personality is the settled framework of reference within which a person addresses the current situation and decides how to behave. Some traits will be dominant at times and then in a balanced relationship to other traits, but each person's traits will be reasonably stable and predictable (see Marshall: 1990 and Seidman: 1994). Hence, once conditioned into a criminal lifestyle, the relevant personality traits are likely to persist until a countervailing conditioning force re-establishes normal social inhibitions. Some forms of criminal behavior such as sexual offences have been medicalized with treatment offered alongside punishment.

Social positivism

1. P. C., brigante della Basilicata, detenuto a Pesaro.
2. Ladro piemontese.
3. Incendiario cieculo di Pesaro, soprannominato *la donna*.
4. Mioden.

In general terms, positivism rejected the Classical Theory's reliance on free will and sought to identify positive causes that determined the propensity for criminal behaviour. The Classical School of Criminology believed that the punishment against a crime, should in fact fit the crime and not be immoderate. This school believes in the fundamental right of equality and that each and every person should be treated the same under the law. Rather than biological or psychological causes, this branch of the School identifies "society" as the cause. Hence, environmental criminology and other sub-schools study the spatial distribution of crimes and offenders (see Adolphe Quetelet, who discovered that crimes rates are relatively constant, and the Chicago School which, under the leadership of Robert E. Park, viewed the city as a form of superorganism, zoned into areas engaged in a continuous process of invasion, dominance, and succession). Meanwhile, Émile Durkheim identified society as a social phenomenon, external to individuals, with crime a normal part of a healthy society. Deviancy was nothing more than "boundary setting," pushing to determine the current limits of morality and acceptability.

Strain Theories

Strain theories state that certain strains or stressors increase the likelihood of crime. These strains involve the inability to achieve one's goals (e.g., monetary or status goals), the loss of positive stimuli (e.g., the death of a friend, the loss of valued possessions), or the presentation of negative stimuli (e.g., verbal and physical abuse). Individuals who experience these strains become upset, and they may turn to crime in an effort to cope. Crime may be a way to reduce or escape from strains.

I. Introduction

Strain theories state that certain strains or stressors increase the likelihood of crime.

These strains involve

- the inability to achieve one's goals (e.g., monetary or status goals),
- the loss of positive stimuli (e.g., the death of a friend, the loss of valued possessions),
- or the presentation of negative stimuli (e.g., verbal and physical abuse).

Individuals who experience these strains become upset, and they may turn to crime in an effort to cope. Crime may be a way to reduce or escape from strains. For example, individuals may steal the money they want or run away from the parents who abuse them. Crime may be used to seek revenge against the source of strain or related targets. For example, individuals may assault the peers who harass them. Crime also may be used to alleviate negative emotions; for example, individuals may engage in illicit drug use in an effort to make themselves feel better. Strain theories are among the dominant explanations of crime, and, as discussed in this research paper, certain strain theories have had a major impact on efforts to control crime.

This research paper describes

- (a) the types of strain most conducive to crime,
- (b) why strains increase the likelihood of crime,
- and (c) the factors that increase the likelihood that individuals will cope with strains through crime.

All strain theories acknowledge that most individuals cope with strains in a legal manner. For example, most individuals cope with monetary problems by doing such things as cutting back on expenses, borrowing money, or working extra hours. It is therefore critical to explain why some individuals engage in criminal coping. After presenting a basic overview of strain theories, this research paper describes how strain theories have been used to explain group differences, such as gender differences, in crime. The research paper concludes with a discussion of the policy implications of strain theories.

II. Types of Strain Most Conducive to Crime

A. Inability to Achieve Monetary Success

Merton (1938) developed the first major strain theory of crime in the 1930s. This theory was developed in the midst of the Great Depression, so it is not surprising that it focused on that type of strain involving the inability to achieve monetary success. According to Merton, everyone in the United Stated—regardless of class position—is encouraged to strive for monetary success. At the same time, lower-class individuals are frequently prevented from achieving such success through legal channels. In particular, the parents of lower-class children often do not equip them with the skills and attitudes necessary to do well in school. Lower-class individuals often attend inferior schools, and they often lack the funds to obtain college educations or start their own businesses. As a consequence, they more often find themselves unable to achieve their monetary goals through legal channels.

This goal blockage creates much frustration, and individuals may cope by engaging in crime, including income-generating crimes such as theft, drug selling, and prostitution. Merton (1938), however, emphasized that most individuals do not cope with this strain through crime. Some individuals simply endure this strain, others lower their desire for money, and still others turn to the pursuit of other goals. Merton provided some guidance as to why some individuals cope with crime and others do not. One key factor, for example, is whether individuals blame their inability to achieve monetary success on themselves or on others. Crime is more likely when the blame is placed on others.

Cohen (1955) and Cloward and Ohlin (1960) have applied Merton's (1938) theory to the explanation of juvenile gangs. Like Merton, they said that the major type of strain in the United States is the inability to achieve monetary success or, in the case of Cohen, the somewhat broader goal of middleclass status. However, they went on to state that juveniles sometimes cope with this strain by forming or joining delinquent groups, such as gangs. Strained juveniles may form gangs in order to better pursue illicit money-making opportunities, such as drug selling. They may form gangs in an effort to achieve the status or respect they desire. In particular, juveniles sometimes join gangs in an effort to feel important.

B. Other Strains Conducive to Crime

Beginning in the 1960s and 1970s, criminologists began to suggest that the inability to achieve monetary success or middle-class status was not the only important type of strain. For example, Greenberg (1977) and Elliott, Huizinga, and Ageton (1979) suggested that juveniles pursue a broad range of goals, including popularity with peers, autonomy from adults, and harmonious relations with parents. They claimed that the inability to achieve any of these goals might result in delinquency. Later, Agnew (1992) drew on the stress literature in psychology and sociology to point to still other types of strain.

According to Agnew (1992), strain refers to events and conditions that are disliked by individuals. These events and conditions may involve the inability to achieve one's goals. As indicated earlier in this research paper, however, strains may also involve the loss of positive stimuli and the presentation of negative stimuli. In more simplistic language, strains involve situations in which individuals (a) lose something good, (b) receive something bad, or (c) cannot get what they want. These ideas formed the basis of Agnew's general strain theory (GST), now the dominant version of strain theory in criminology.

Literally hundreds of specific strains fall under the three broad categories of strain listed in GST. Not all of these strains are conducive to crime, however. For example, homelessness is a type of strain that is very conducive to crime. Being placed in "time out" by one's parents for misbehaving is a type of strain that is not conducive to crime. GST states that strains are most likely to lead to crime when they (a) are high in magnitude, (b) are perceived as unjust, (c) are associated with low social control (or with little to lose from crime), and (d) create some pressure or incentive for criminal coping (see Agnew, 2006). Homelessness is clearly conducive to crime: It is high in magnitude, often perceived as unjust, and associated with low social control (individuals who are homeless have little to lose by engaging in crime). Furthermore, being homeless creates much pressure to engage in crime, because one must often steal to meet basic needs and engage in violence to protect oneself (see Baron, 2004). Being placed in time out for misbehavior has none of these characteristics.

GST lists the strains most likely to result in crime. These include the inability to achieve monetary goals as well as a good number of other strains. In particular, the following specific strains are most likely to result in crime:

- **Parental rejection**. Parents do not express love or affection for their children, show little interest in them, and provide little support to them.

- **Harsh/excessive/unfair discipline**. Such discipline involves physical punishment, the use of humiliation and insults, screaming, and threats of injury. Also, such discipline is excessive given the nature of the infraction or when individuals are disciplined when they do not deserve it.

- **Child abuse and neglect**. This includes physical abuse; sexual abuse; emotional abuse; and the failure to provide adequate food, shelter, or medical care.

- **Negative school experiences**. These include low grades, negative relations with teachers (e.g., teachers treat the juvenile unfairly, humiliate or belittle the juvenile), and the experience of school as boring and a waste of time.

- **Abusive peer relations**. Peer abuse includes insults, gossip, threats, attempts to coerce, and physical assaults.

- **Work in "bad" jobs**. Such jobs have low pay, little prestige, few benefits, little opportunity for advancement, coercive control (e.g., threats of being fired), and unpleasant working conditions (e.g., simple, repetitive tasks; little autonomy; physically taxing work).

- **Unemployment**, especially when it is chronic and blamed on others.
- **Marital problems**, including frequent conflicts and verbal and physical abuse.
- **Criminal victimization**.
- **Discrimination** based on race/ethnicity, gender, or religion.
- **Homelessness**.
- **Failure** to achieve certain goals, including thrills/excitement, high levels of autonomy, masculine status, and monetary goals.

C. Research on Strains and Crime

Researchers have examined the effect of most of the preceding strains on crime. Their studies suggest that these strains do increase the likelihood of crime, with certain of them being among the most important causes of crime (see Agnew, 2006, for an overview). For example, parental rejection, harsh discipline, criminal victimization, and homelessness have all been found to have relatively large effects on crime. The following are two examples of recent research in this area. Spano, Riveria, and Bolland (2006) found that juveniles who were violently victimized were much more likely to engage in subsequent violence. This held true even after they took account of such things as the juvenile's sex, age, prior level of violence, level of parental monitoring, and whether the juvenile belonged to a gang. Baron (2004) studied a sample of homeless street youth in a Canadian city and found that crime was much more common among youth who reported that they had been homeless for many months in the prior year. This finding was true even after a broad range of other factors were taken into account, such as age, gender, and criminal peer association.

Labeling theory

Sarah
Part II

Introduction

Labeling theory is a vibrant area of research and theoretical development within the field of criminology. Originating in the mid- to late-1960s in the United States at a moment of tremendous political and cultural conflict, labeling theorists brought to center stage the role of government agencies, and social processes in general, in the creation of deviance and crime. The theory represented both a theoretical and methodological break from the past, and it could reasonably be argued that it was one of the dominant theoretical perspectives in the study of crime and deviance from the late 1960s until the early 1980s. It was also responsible for spurring countless empirical studies over this time period. Although there were periods when interest in labeling process was in decline, particularly after 1985, labeling theory has had a bit of a resurgence in recent years. Labeling theory has become part of a more general criminological theory of sanctions that includes deterrence theory's focus on the crime reduction possibilities of sanctions, procedural justice theory's focus on the importance of the manner in which sanctions are imposed, and defiance/reintegrative theory's emphasis on individual differences in the social bond and persons' emotional reaction to the label. Labeling theories of crime are often referred to as social reaction theories, because they focus primarily on the consequences of responses or reactions to crime. These responses or reactions typically focus on three sets of actors: (1) informal social others, such as the friends, parents, or partners of persons committing crimes, and who disapprove of the offender's behavior; (2) organizations or institutions such as the criminal justice system, whose function it is to "do something about" crime; and (3) those who perceive a threat by some behavior and want to see legislation passed to outlaw it. All of these very diverse actions have one thing in common: they are all reactions to crime. As such, they are said to be "labels" because they have the quality of attaching a name or a signature to someone or some behavior—hence the name "labeling theory." From this, labeling theory can be understood as involving two main hypotheses. First is the status characteristics hypothesis, which states that labels are imposed in part because of the status of those doing the labeling and those being labeled. The second is the secondary deviance hypothesis, which essentially argues that deviant labels create problems that the one being labeled must adjust to and deal with, and that under certain conditions labels can lead to greater involvement in crime and deviance.

General Overviews

Since the advent of the "positive school" of criminology, beginning with the work of Cesare Lombroso in the late 1800s, scholars of crime have been primarily interested in studying what factors cause individuals to commit acts of crime and deviance. Whether the causal factors are biological (e.g., atavism), psychological (e.g., impulsivity), or sociological (e.g., bad peers or neighborhoods), the scientific study of crime and deviance has, for the most part, focused on those factors that produce it, and on the essential differences between the "normal" and the "deviant." Labeling theory brought a fresh, new perspective to this point of view. Labeling theorists are generally uninterested in the causes of crime, and are more interested in the reactions to crime. These reactions to crime, or labels, occur in processes at different levels of aggregation—the individual, the institutional, and the macro (state or national rule making)—and how labeled persons respond to those labels. The unique theoretical positions that labeling theory offered about crime and deviance can best be understood by careful reading of some "primary sources." One of these sources is Lemert 1951, a general treatment of social problems and social deviance that first introduced the theoretical importance of the distinction between primary and secondary deviance. Lemert's work would later prove to be a valuable theoretical foundation for labeling theories of general deviance, but it was Becker 1963 that would be more influential to criminologists, because it laid out, in very clear form, labeling theory positions on the nature of deviant acts, how some behaviors get to be labeled as deviant, and what happens when persons are labeled as deviant. In the early- to mid-1960s, labeling theorists published numerous theoretical works and influenced a great deal of empirical work. By the 1980s, however, critics began to seriously question the validity of labeling theory, primarily on the grounds that the empirical research did not seem to confirm the two major labeling propositions. Tittle 1980 is illustrative of this position; Tittle argues that if labeling theory claims only that status characteristics have some effect, then the theory is unimportant, and if it fails to be clear about the magnitude of the effect, then it is imprecise. Although the dominance once enjoyed by the theory waned considerably, theoretical and empirical work in the late 1980s and early 1990s revitalized the theory and integrated labeling propositions into more general theories of crime. See also Paternoster and Iovanni 1989 and Braithwaite 1989.

Routine activities theory

Diagram: Triangle labeled "Routine Activities Theory" with three surrounding labels — "Motivated Offender", "Suitable target", and "Absence of capable guardian".

Routine activities theory is a theory of crime events. This differs from a majority of criminological theories, which focus on explaining why some people commit crimes—that is, the motivation to commit crime— rather than how criminal events are produced. Although at first glance this distinction may appear inconsequential, it has important implications for the research and prevention of crime. Routine activities theory suggests that the organization of routine activities in society create opportunities for crime.

Routine activities theory suggests that the organization of routine activities in society create opportunities for crime. In other words, the daily routine activities of people—including where they work, the routes they travel to and from school, the groups with whom the socialize, the shops they frequent, and so forth—strongly influence when, where, and to whom crime occurs.

These routines can make crime easy and low risk, or difficult and risky. Because opportunities vary over time, space, and among people, so too does the likelihood of crime. Therefore, research that stems from routine activities theory generally examines various opportunity structures that facilitate crime; prevention strategies that are informed by routine activities theory attempt to alter these opportunity structures to prevent criminal events.

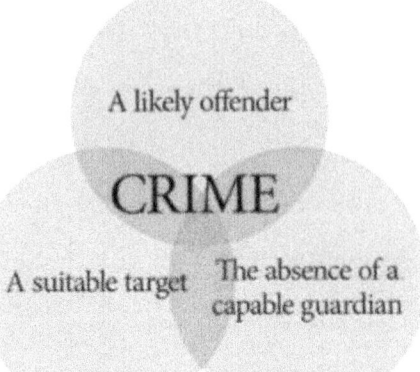

A likely offender

CRIME

A suitable target   The absence of a capable guardian

Routine activities theory was initially used to explain changes in crime trends over time. It has been increasingly used much more broadly to understand and prevent crime problems. Researchers have used various methods to test hypotheses derived from the theory. Since its inception, the theory has become closely aligned with a set of theories and perspectives known as environmental criminology, which focuses on the importance of opportunity in determining the distribution of crime across time and space.

Environmental criminology, and routine activities theory in particular, has very practical implications for prevention; therefore, practitioners have applied routine activities theory to inform police practices and prevention strategies. This research paper contains a review of the evolution of routine activities theory; a summary of research informed by the theory; complementary perspectives and current applications; and future directions for theory, research, and prevention.

Theory

In 1979, Cohen and Felson questioned why urban crime rates increased during the 1960s, when the factors commonly thought to cause violent crime, such as poor economic conditions, had generally improved during this time. Cohen and Felson (1979) suggested that a crime should be thought of as an event that occurs at a specific location and time and involves specific people and/or objects. They argued that crime events required three minimal elements to converge in time and space: (1) an offender who was prepared to commit the offense; (2) a suitable target, such as a human victim to be assaulted or a piece of property to be stolen; and (3) the absence of a guardian capable of preventing the crime. The lack of any of these three elements, they argued, would be sufficient to prevent a crime event from occurring. Drawing from human ecological theories, Cohen and Felson suggested that structural changes in societal routine activity patterns can influence crime rates by affecting the likelihood of the convergence in time and space of these three necessary elements. As the routine activities of people change, the likelihood of targets converging in time and space with motivated offenders without guardians also changes. In other words, opportunities for crime—and, in turn, crime patterns—are a function of the routine activity patterns in society.

Cohen and Felson (1979) argued that crime rates increased after World War II because the routine activities of society had begun to shift away from the home, thus increasing the likelihood that motivated offenders would converge in time and space with suitable targets in the absence of capable guardianship. Routine activities that take place at or near the home tend to be associated with more guardianship—for both the individual and his or her property—and a lower risk of encountering potential offenders. When people perform routine activities away from the home, they are more likely to encounter potential offenders in the absence of guardians. Furthermore, their belongings in their home are left unguarded, thus creating more opportunities for crime to take place.

One of the greatest contributions of routine activities theory is the idea that criminal opportunities are not spread evenly throughout society; neither are they infinite. Instead, there is some limit on the number of available targets viewed as attractive/suitable by the offender. Cohen and Felson (1979) suggested that suitability is a function of at least four qualities of the target: Value, Inertia, Visibility, and Access, or VIVA. All else being equal, those persons or products that are repeatedly targeted will have the following qualities: perceived value by the offender, either material or symbolic; size and weight that makes the illegal treatment possible; physically visible to potential offenders; and accessible to offenders. Cohen and Felson argued that two additional societal trends—the increase in sales of consumer goods and the design of small durable products—were affecting the crime by means of the supply of suitable targets. These trends in society increased the supply of suitable targets available and, in turn, the likelihood of crime. As the supply of small durable goods continued to rise, the level of suitable targets also rose, thus increasing the number of available criminal opportunities.

Since its inception, routine activities theory has been developed to further specify the necessary elements for a criminal event and those that have the potential to prevent it. The people who prevent crime have been subdivided according to whom or what they are supervising—offender, target, or place—and are now collectively referred to as controllers. Handlers are people who exert informal social control over potential offenders to prevent them from committing crimes (Felson, 1986). Examples of handlers include parents who chaperone their teenager's social gatherings, a probation officer who supervises probationers, and a school resource officer who keeps an eye on school bullies. Handlers have some sort of personal connection with the potential offenders. Their principal interest is in keeping the potential offender out of trouble. Guardians protect suitable targets from offenders (Cohen & Felson, 1979). Examples of guardians include the owner of a car who locks his vehicle, a child care provider who keeps close watch over the children in public, and a coworker who walks another to his car in the parking garage. The principal interest of guardians is the protection of their potential targets. Finally, managers supervise and monitor specific places (Eck, 1994). Place managers might include the owner of a shop who installs surveillance cameras, an apartment landlord who updates the locks on the doors, and park rangers who enforce littering codes. The principal interest of managers is the functioning of places.

Choice Theory

Overview of Choice Theory

- Belonging
- Power
- Freedom
- Fun
- Survival

Quality World → Perceived World → (Knowledge filter) → (Value filter) → The Real World

Comparing Place — Total Behavior Car

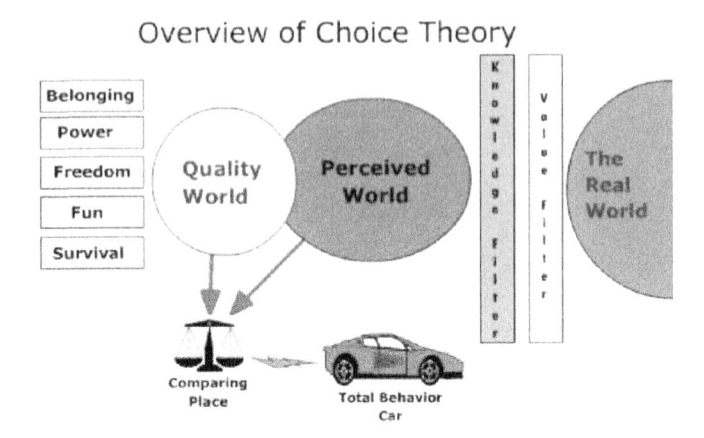

Choice theory contends that we are internally motivated, not externally motivated by rewards and punishment.

Originally called "control theory," Glasser switched to "choice theory" in 1996 to emphasize that virtually all behavior is chosen.

CHOICE THEORY: WHAT MOTIVATES US?

Choice theory represents an alternative to behaviorism and other external control psychologies.

Rather than seeing people as "shaped" by rewards and punishment, Choice Theory suggests that we always have some capacity to make choices and exercise control in our lives.

Choice Theory teaches that we are always motivated by what we want at that moment. It emphasizes the importance of building and maintaining positive relationships with others to create a shared vision. People who develop shared **"quality world pictures"** are motivated to pursue common goals and are more likely to work collaboratively.

CHOICE THEORY SUMMARY

A basic understanding of Choice Theory requires some knowledge of the following 5 key concepts:

1. Basic Needs

2. The Quality World

3. Reality & Perception

4. Comparing Place

5. Total Behavior

Choice Theory: The Basic Needs

All people are born with 5 basic needs:

1. to love & belong

2. to be powerful

3. to be free

4. to have fun

5. to survive

All behavior is purposeful, motivated by our incessant desire to satisfy the basic needs woven into our genes.

The strength of each need varies from person to person.

For example, some are more driven by the social need to love and belong while others are more driven by the need to be free and autonomous.

1. Choice Theory: The Quality World

Each of us develops a unique Quality World, the source of all motivation.

Whereas the Basic Needs represent "nature," The Quality World represents "nurture." As we live our lives and interact with others, we each build this unique Quality World that includes the people, activities, values, and beliefs that are most important to us as individuals.

Everything we place in our Quality World is need satisfying.

Examples:

- I love these people.

- I feel a sense of power when I am singing on stage.

- I have fun when I am playing outside with my children.

Throughout our lives, we add and delete "pictures" from our Quality World. Some people develop Quality World pictures that are unhealthy and irresponsible.

Examples:

- Think of people who only feel a sense of power or freedom when drinking alcohol or taking other drugs.

- Think of people who have fun when hurting others physically or emotionally.

Choice Theory suggests that parents, educators, and the community at large can promote environments that encourage others to develop Quality World pictures that let them satisfy their needs responsibly.

2. Choice Theory: Reality & Perception

Even though we all live in the Real World, Choice Theory contends that what matters is our perception of reality.

We behave based on what we perceive to be real, whether we are right or wrong.

Choice Theory states that information passes through three distinct filters as we create our perception of reality:

1. the sensory filter

2. the knowledge filter

3. the value filter

Because of these filters, two or more people may witness the same event or participate in the same activity and develop radically different perceptions.

Examples:

- We may all agree that Barack Obama is president of the United States, but there are multiple perceptions about how "good" or bad" a president he is.

- Talk to a couple of Red Sox and Yankee fans and you'll quickly understand that the same "real world" is perceived very differently because of their value filters.

3. Choice Theory: The Comparing Place

Our brain continually compares two images:

1. our perception of reality

2. our Quality World picture of what we want at that moment

The purpose of all behavior is to create a match between what we perceive and what we want.

When there is a match, we will maintain the behaviors we have chosen. When there is enough of a mismatch to cause internal discomfort, we automatically search for new behaviors that will create the match we seek.

Examples:

- A classroom teacher looks around the room and notices that the students are actively involved in the activity she has asked them to do. She gets a positive internal signal and continues her current teaching strategies

- A parent notices that their child is behaving poorly at home and in school. The mismatch between what the parent wants and what they perceive leads them to try new strategies designed to help the child behave more responsibly.

4. Choice Theory: Total Behavior

All behavior has four components:

1. acting

2. thinking

3. feeling

4. physiology

When we change any one component of behavior, the other components change as well.

The two easiest components to control directly are acting and thinking. It is virtually impossible to change your feelings or physiology directly.

Examples:

- Imagine you could feel less sad or depressed just because you wanted to.
- Imagine a student who is agitated and frustrated and could just calm down because he wanted to.

Since all four components work in concert, however, we have much more control over our feelings and physiology than we realize. By choosing to act and/or think differently, our feelings and physiology automatically change.

Practitioners of Choice Theory help people choose responsible actions and thoughts that lead them to feel better and positively impact their physiology.

HOW CHOICE THEORY IMPACTS LEARNING

When Choice Theory is applied in the classroom, as it has been in schools across the world, it has a significant impact on how instruction is delivered.

The Teacher As Manager

The role of the teacher/manager is to help students see that working hard and doing what the teacher asks is worth the effort and will add quality to their lives. This is achieved by developing positive relationships with students and providing active, relevant learning experiences where students can demonstrate success.

Effective teacher/managers create shared Quality World pictures with their students so students are motivated to learn what the teacher wants to teach.

The Needs-Satisfying Classroom

When creating lessons, teachers who practice Choice Theory ensure that students can satisfy their needs by doing what the teacher asks them to do.

Learning increases and disruption diminishes when students know that they are able to connect, feel a sense of competence and power, have some freedom, and enjoy themselves in a safe, secure environment. (Chapter 10 of The Motivated Student: Unlocking the Enthusiasm for Learning offers a specific strategy that helps teachers plan lessons with their students' needs in mind)

Common Characteristics

Classrooms and schools that apply Choice Theory share the following 3 characteristics:

1. **Coercion is minimized**. Rather than trying to "make" students behave by using rewards and punishments, teachers build positive relationships with their students, managing them without coercion. Coercion never inspires quality.

2. **Focus on quality**. Teachers expect mastery of concepts and encourage students to re-take tests and continue to work on assignments until they have demonstrated competence or quality. The emphasis is on deep learning demonstrated through the ability to apply what has been learned.

3. **Self-evaluation**. Self-evaluation is a cornerstone of Choice Theory. Given helpful information (rubrics, models, exemplars, etc.) students take on greater ownership of their learning by evaluating their own performance routinely. Encouraging students to self-evaluate promotes responsibility and helps students pursue goals and become skilled decision-makers because they are more actively involved in their education.

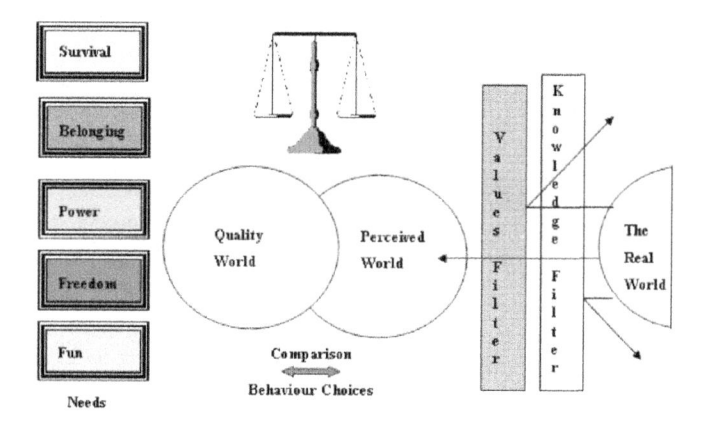

Psychological Theories of Crime

Introduction

Why do individuals commit crimes? At the same time, why is crime present in our society? The criminal justice system is very concerned with these questions, and criminologists are attempting to answer them. In actuality, the question of why crime is committed is very difficult to answer. However, for centuries, people have been searching for answers (Jacoby, 2004). It is important to recognize that there are many different explanations as to why individuals commit crime (Conklin, 2007). One of the main explanations is based on psychological theories, which focus on the association among intelligence, personality, learning, and criminal behavior. Thus, in any discussion concerning crime causation, one must contemplate psychological theories.

When examining psychological theories of crime, one must be cognizant of the three major theories. The first is psychodynamic theory, which is centered on the notion that an individual's early childhood experience influences his or her likelihood for committing future crimes. The second is behavioral theory. Behavioral theorists have expanded the work of Gabriel Tarde through behavior modeling and social learning. The third is cognitive theory, the major premise of which suggests that an individual's perception and how it is manifested (Jacoby, 2004) affect his or her potential to commit crime. In other words, behavioral theory focuses on how an individual's perception of the world influences his or her behavior.

Also germane to psychological theories are personality and intelligence. Combined, these five theories or characteristics (i.e., psychodynamic, cognitive, behavioral, personality, and intelligence) offer appealing insights into why an individual may commit a crime (Schmalleger, 2008). However, one should not assume this there is only one reason why a person commits crime. Researchers looking for a single explanation should be cautious, because there is no panacea for the problem of crime.

2. Early Research

Charles Goring (1870–1919) discovered a relationship between crime and flawed intelligence. Goring examined more than 3,000 convicts in England. It is important to note that Goring found no physical differences between noncriminals and criminals; however, he did find that criminals are more likely to be insane, to be unintelligent, and to exhibit poor social behavior. A second pioneer is Gabriel Tarde (1843–1904), who maintained that individuals learn from each other and ultimately imitate one another. Interestingly, Tarde thought that out of 100 individuals, only 1 was creative or inventive and the remainder were prone to imitation (Jacoby, 2004).

3. Psychodynamic Theory

Proponents of psychodynamic theory suggest that an individual's personality is controlled by unconscious mental processes that are grounded in early childhood. This theory was originated by Sigmund Freud (1856–1939), the founder of psychoanalysis. Imperative to this theory are the three elements or structures that make up the human personality: (1) the id, (2), the ego, and (3) the superego. One can think of the id is as the primitive part of a person's mental makeup that is present at birth. Freud (1933) believed the id represents the unconscious biological drives for food, sex, and other necessities over the life span. Most important is the idea that the id is concerned with instant pleasure or gratification while disregarding concern for others. This is known as the pleasure principle, and it is often paramount when discussing criminal behavior. All too often, one sees news stories and studies about criminal offenders who have no concern for anyone but themselves. Is it possiblethat these male and female offenders are driven by instant gratification? The second element of the human personality is the ego, which is thought to develop early in a person's life. For example, when children learn that their wishes cannot be gratified instantaneously, they often throw a tantrum. Freud (1933) suggested that the ego compensates for the demands of the id by guiding an individual's actions or behaviors to keep him or her within the boundaries of society. The ego is guided by the reality principle. The third element of personality, the superego, develops as a person incorporates the moral standards and values of the community; parents; and significant others, such as friends and clergy members. The focus of the superego is morality. The superego serves to pass judgment on the behavior and actions of individuals (Freud, 1933). The ego mediates between the id's desire for instant gratification and the strict morality of the superego. One can assume that young adults as well as adults understand right from wrong. However, when a crime is committed, advocates of psychodynamic theory would suggest that an individual committed a crime because he or she has an underdeveloped superego.

In sum, psychodynamic theory suggests that criminal offenders are frustrated and aggravated. They are constantly drawn to past events that occurred in their early childhood. Because of a negligent, unhappy, or miserable childhood, which is most often characterized by a lack of love and/or nurturing, a criminal offender has a weak (or absent) ego. Most important, research suggests that having a weak ego is linked with poor or absence of social etiquette, immaturity, and dependence on others. Research further suggests that individuals with weak egos may be more likely to engage in drug abuse.

Recognize the Signs That Someone Is Lying

Lying and deception are common human behaviors. Until relatively recently, there has been little actual research into just how often people lie. A 2004 Reader's Digest poll found that as many as 96% of people admit to lying at least sometimes.[1]

One national study published in 2009 surveyed 1,000 U.S. adults and found that 60% of respondents claimed that they did not lie at all. Instead, the researchers found that about half of all lies were told by just 5% of all the subjects.[2] The study suggests that while prevalence rates may vary, there likely exists a small group of very prolific liars.

The reality is that most people will probably lie from time to time. Some of these lies are little white lies intended to protect someone else's feelings ("No, that shirt does not make you look fat!"). In other cases, these lies can be much more serious (like lying on a resume) or even sinister (covering up a crime).

Lying Can Be Hard to Detect

People are surprisingly bad at detecting lies. One study, for example, found that people were only able to accurately detect lying 54% of the time in a lab setting—hardly impressive when factoring in a 50% detection rate by pure chance alone.[3]

Clearly, behavioral differences between honest and lying individuals are difficult to discriminate and measure. Researchers have attempted to uncover different ways of detecting lies. While there may not be a simple, tell-tale sign that someone is dishonest (like Pinocchio's nose), researchers have found a few helpful indicators.

Like many things, though, detecting a lie often comes down to one thing—trusting your instincts. By knowing what signs might accurately detect a lie and learning how to heed your own gut reactions, you may be able to become better at spotting falsehoods.

Signs of Lying

Psychologists have utilized research on body language and deception to help members of law enforcement distinguish between the truth and lies. Researchers at UCLA conducted studies on the subject in addition to analyzing 60 studies on deception in order to develop recommendations and training for law enforcement. The results of their research were published in the *American Journal of Forensic Psychiatry*.[4]

Red Flags That Someone May Be Lying

A few of the potential red flags the researchers identified that might indicate that people are deceptive include:

- Being vague; offering few details
- Repeating questions before answering them
- Speaking in sentence fragments
- Failing to provide specific details when a story is challenged
- Grooming behaviors such as playing with hair or pressing fingers to lips

Lead researcher R. Edward Geiselman suggests that while detecting deception is never easy, quality training can improve a person's ability to detect lies:

"Without training, many people think they can detect deception, but their perceptions are unrelated to their actual ability. Quick, inadequate training sessions lead people to over-analyze and to do worse than if they go with their gut reactions."[4]

Tips for Identifying Lying

If you suspect that someone might not be telling the truth, there are a few strategies you can use that might help distinguish fact from fiction.

Don't Rely on Body Language Alone

When it comes to detecting lies, people often focus on body language "tells," or subtle physical and behavioral signs that reveal deception. While body language cues can sometimes hint at deception, research suggests that many expected behaviors are not always associated with lying.[5]

Researcher Howard Ehrlichman, a psychologist who has been studying eye movements since the 1970s, has found that eye movements do not signify lying at all. In fact, he suggests that shifting eyes mean that a person is thinking, or more precisely, that he or she is accessing their long-term memory.[6]

Other studies have shown that while individual signals and behaviors are useful indicators of deception, some of the ones most often linked to lying (such as eye movements) are among the worst predictors.[7] So while body language can be a useful tool in the detection of lies, the key is to understand which signals to pay attention to.

Focus On the Right Signals

One meta-analysis found that while people do often rely on valid cues for detecting lies, the problem might lie with the weakness of these cues as deception indicators in the first place.[3]

Some of the most accurate deception cues that people do pay attention to include:

- **Being vague:** If the speaker seems to intentionally leave out important details, it might be because they are lying.

- **Vocal uncertainty:** If the person seems unsure or insecure, they are more likely to be perceived as lying.

- **Indifference:** Shrugging, lack of expression, and a bored posture can be signs of lying since the person is trying to avoid conveying emotions and possible tells.

- **Overthinking:** If the individual seems to be thinking too hard to fill in the details of the story, it might be because they are deceiving you.

The lesson here is that while body language may be helpful, it is important to pay attention to the right signals. However, some experts suggest that relying too heavily on certain signals may impair the ability to detect lies.[8]

Ask Them to Tell Their Story in Reverse

Lie detection can be seen as a passive process. People may assume they can just observe the potential liar's body language and facial expressions to spot obvious "tells." In taking a more active approach to uncovering lies, you can yield better results.

Some research has suggested that asking people to report their stories in reverse order rather than chronological order can increase the accuracy of lie detection. Verbal and non-verbal cues that distinguish between lying and truth-telling may become more apparent as cognitive load increases.[9]

Lying is more mentally taxing than telling the truth. If you add even more cognitive complexity, behavioral cues may become more apparent.

Not only is telling a lie more cognitively demanding, but liars typically exert much more mental energy toward monitoring their behaviors and evaluating the responses of others. They are concerned with their credibility and ensuring that other people believe their stories. All this takes a considerable amount of effort, so if you throw in a difficult task (like relating their story in reverse order), cracks in the story and other behavioral indicators might become easier to spot.

In one study, 80 mock suspects either told the truth or lied about a staged event. Some of the individuals were asked to report their stories in reverse order while others simply told their stories in chronological order. The researchers found that the reverse order interviews revealed more behavioral clues to deception.[10]

In a second experiment, 55 police officers watched taped interviews from the first experiment and were asked to determine who was lying and who was not. The investigation revealed that law enforcement officers were better at detecting lies in the reverse order interviews than they were in the chronological interviews.[10]

Trust Your Instincts

Your immediate gut reactions might be more accurate than any conscious lie detection you might attempt. In one study, researchers had 72 participants watch videos of interviews with mock crime suspects.[11] Some of these suspects had stolen a $100 bill from off a bookshelf while others had not, yet all of the suspects were told to tell the interviewer that they had not taken the money.

Similar to previous studies, the participants were unable to consistently detect lies, only accurately identifying the liars 43% of the time and the truth-tellers 48% of the time.[11]

But the researchers also utilized implicit behavioral reaction time tests to assess the participants' more automatic and unconscious responses to the suspects. What they discovered was that the subjects were more likely to unconsciously associate words like "dishonest" and "deceitful" with the suspects that were actually lying.[11] They were also more likely to implicitly associate words like "valid" and "honest" with the truth-tellers.

The results suggest that people may have an unconscious, intuitive idea about whether someone is lying.

So if our gut reactions might be more accurate, why are people not better at identifying dishonesty? Conscious responses might interfere with our automatic associations. Instead of relying on our instincts, people focus on the stereotypical behaviors that they often associate with lying such as fidgeting and lack of eye contact.[7] Overemphasizing behaviors that unreliably predict deceptions makes it more difficult to distinguish between truth and lies.

A Word From Verywell

The reality is that there is no universal, surefire sign that someone is lying. All of the signs, behaviors, and indicators that researchers have linked to lying are simply clues that *might* reveal whether a person is being forthright.

Next time you are trying to gauge the veracity of an individual's story, stop looking at the clichéd "lying signs" and learn how to spot more subtle behaviors that might be linked to deception. When necessary, take a more active approach by adding pressure and make telling the lie more mentally taxing by asking the speaker to relate the story in reverse order.

Finally, and perhaps most importantly, trust your instincts. You might have a great intuitive sense of honesty versus dishonesty. Learn to heed those gut feelings.

Printed in Great Britain
by Amazon